T0043386

# My Letter to God

# My Letter to God

*Listen To Me and Listen to Me Good*

DANYELL TODD

Rev. date: 05/19/2020

**To order additional copies of this book, contact:**
Xlibris
1-888-795-4274
www.Xlibris.com
Orders@Xlibris.com
811052

# Contents

# Number 8

Dear God sometimes I wonder who you really are and why does life feel like a number eight. Its like repeated cycles from generation to generation; at the top you feel so relieved of the reality to come. But the bottom you feel six feet under, and the middle of life you feel all on top and bottom hurt, pain, ups, downs and the bitterness of being a survivor. I once heard a conversation at the last funeral I attended when someone mentioned "not to never question God". Now I withdrew myself from the conversation because I've asked you multiple of questions and you answered me. Nature not only nature but you allow people, places and things to enter our life's purpose. Learning challenges that way we know the difference between the answer we got and the questioned we asked.

Now I've recently learned that life is an emotional battle whatever you decide to give your emotions to become your mind. Emotions are revised into something much bigger than love. If you had an revival movement in your life that felt academic and there was an emotion

behind it. I'm sure cleaning out your closet will courageously change the inside. Now love the other hand come's with different mountains, heavy barriers and a whole lot of climbing. But why must love be hard if you're the God of love? Didn't you create love in our daily lives as the sunset and sunrise.

The energy of love, peace, and fantastic emotion is staring me right in my eyes. Sun gazing while practicing how to be sensitive to stress and depression; physically and mentally as well. Its love that captures my attention as you light-fully light my light. Modeling as you in a world of unbelief because of the falling meteorite. Surviving the pathways of this earth as I strike the ground high speed causing a heat up and a glow. Now God you know its hard shinning this bright with frowns from family yea right. Too much envy for all of us to have the same blood type.

Obtaining many of planets and different stars queen of the under world right from the start. I'll let the earth be my celestial body moving in an elliptical orbit around the star. Blending in with dissimilar people judging; and not the star. You know that luminous point in life where your incandescent body shine like the sun just by night. But which am I? How do I multitask different faces? In a world of people with different opinions about your spirit and how your living.

Speak through me and not like the drug society use to cure pain physically. They're dedicated to medicated pills and portions while screaming on the inside for help of pain. Beasting bones and joints for a high point aiming like a star. God is that you taping into the people hearts? Healing and stitching scars; eyes closed seeing many different stars. Where are you God? How much higher? High above the universe and body can't make it this far. Your soul is your aiming sphere while standing at one point as a Giza Pyramid.

# Epiphany

Dear God how did this happen? How did I spiritually see the reality of my life unfolding right before my eyes. God is this explainable your spirit living and speaking in human form. Multitasking the living from the dead allowing man to meet you before they actually meet you. Energy, frequency and vibration invisibly controls the here and now. Universal technique's making thundering sounds as hidden objects watch over the earth. Waiting to swipe out mankind with forces vs powers devastating to no one by a lack of concern. Knowledge has been favorable and without it the tree of life is rootless.

God of billions of roots genetic molecules controlling the chemical reaction of life. But when mixing different chromosomes wrongfully immature beings was brought in to change the pattern of life on earth. Which explains why this generation of people leave earth before they're great grand parents and regular parent's. Species of planets known and unknown to produce a concept of God one for the people and one not. Spiritually time traveling from one place

to another. Omnipresent knowing that you've lived and relived a moment of deja-vu God is that you within me as a tool.

Experimenting many functions and scientific methods to know self; I've equipped my spirit for the magical moment that's inside of me. Writing this letter with the best side of me star Capella dazzling like two. God I am that I am and that make you not for me but for you. A Greater future standing on success while tomorrow I feel beyond blessed. Not in worry by the days; a quick awakening about all of my stays. A world of foreign gun play still my soul refuse to be betrayed. Teleporting the moon from the sun I myself has to get this done.

Transporting across space and distance instantly I see a center providing interconnections between different forms of telecommunications. Especially one which links satellite and ground-based communications. God is this how you reach us as your inner being's. That's mighty speaking, loudly and commanding true knowledge to be heard. Generosity carried like balance the key to life weighing in as one another. Cubic meters and measurements of the same; equally out to be one. People and animals mistreated like is that's not called love.

Glassed eye vision only seeing one space; like eagles transformed living many long lives. Geniusly I've mastered the here and now outliving many of those to come. A before and after time being of some; God it's you that orbit planets and people to come. Hidden in many places throughout the world like knowledge of forever time and that's our time. A time to live and not die dedicated to the most high me vs me & that's no lie. Inside of people testing energy like alkaline. Now read in between those lines were people used lines instead of getting baptized.

# Meditation

Dear God I need another way of communicating with you; I mean like another way to tap into you. Something soothing but nurturing as well helping me channel unwanted energy. Just spending quality time with self and balancing complicated emotions of the world. Not having to adjust destruction but cooperate with nature. Involving from a caterpillar to a butterfly flying from life to flower to bloom. Realizing that having the ability to take action and speak over people does not always make you a good leader. Only a tyrant.

Meditation father it's our time with one another's energy challenge by an out pouring of good vibration. Why must I have to face the cruel and oppressive ruler. Running in and out of churches looking for a existing being that isn't you. Not like that don't find this misconstrued. Wrong face on a planet that's our place. So many fragile from the past more like a retrace.

We've all heard that if you can win the morning you can win the day. One way of doing that that is too create regular rituals and

routines; so you don't have to think about what you need to do for the day, future, etc. It's science momentum and beneficial as opposed to being reactive, like how a lot of people do. For instance 85% of Americans grab their phone as soon as they awaken in the mourning. Not proactively spending time with self care, self love a vision and a direction for the day. How you do anything is how you do everything therefore have mindfulness so that way your mind is clear enough to enter into the day. Not with said the negatives that you face can instantly be turned positive.

I do believe in cold therapy because it helps to reset your nervous system. Powerful ice bath reduces inflammation that's in different area's of the body. I also believe in the cold water fast just water fill ups every time a hungry come about. It helps the brain to process more energy that's convenient for self. But father meditation has quickened my godly powers while churches proceed to tell us that godly powers are located in church only. Confusing to your people that have a lack of knowledge. How would they understand they're true meditative self that increases powers within? Listen to me and listen to me Good.

Powers has struggles that becomes afflicted with higher self. Being able to know the know how has a different effect on each one of us as individual's foreign vibration. Least we all be of the same kind to make the enemy know his kind of blood typed. Feet and blood type stamped at birth to know who's easily destroyed and who's not. Of course, we all shall go on powerless after the battles and daily confusing energy of our enemy tactfulness. Weighing in as opponents of each other less problems can be presented in a world pf powers. Yes, all is power above & beyond the universe.

# It Bothers Me

God it really bothers me to see so many under age female's motherless while loveless. How did you create the women body as perfection. Yet again more women feel drawn to selling they're bodies as a token success. Pure Gold shining while being stolen from the pyramids. To each it's own used or misused valued in between low balance. God why have these enemy's created such a challenge; with teachings of the wrong ying-yang. Down grading women a black men has made an all time high. Not that high I mean yes that high being controlled and trying to control.

A chemical blast as if mars doesn't have a free space. Just 250 million miles away were rockets u turn and doesn't keep straight. So much for real estate that way we may never escape. Our red planet were life was originated for scientific beings out of the periodic table. Genetically engineered for extant life to those that have a knowing of self. God now I know life is beyond the human brain operating like

the universe. The conqueror and God of war Ares structured with realizations and that's mind for Gold.

Yea mind is gold but yet again it's easy to be controlled. Pills and possession maybe even NASA, inhabit living organism. But God who belong to you? A question for the world and you just like a nerve under depression in a cell of a crew. Descendants of Martians who were once blue. Mars is that you because our enemy will do anything to portray you. In a circled radius repeated with frequency, energy and vibration. That's earth the smallest planet in space so I'll rather live life without a trace.

Bothered and unbothered I have my crew mutual in love while followings after me. As if they hate me but love me; with a difference in between the two. Me vs me like planet Nibiru; gracefully moving destructive energy from afar like a Goddess will do. Why bother now even Almighty origin of love was millions years ago. God now I know what to look for so that I don't overlook anything. Patient like a butterfly taken my time to grow in this not so act of life or role. But I'm just now breaking through the cocoon gaining a new set of wings for growth and control.

Mark of the bat because the enemy is dark inside. Watch the eye for fluoride dried out by so much pride. How about a karmic resolution to avoid any cost of the constitution. Now I'm flying limited edition; best days ever authentic. Yes, I'm facing the wind like before and you granted my wish and let me explore. Enough is enough like a lion's roar. Take flight read on and get ready to restore.

# Third Eye

Dear God oh how fearful I was to be able to comprehend my third eye. It's like reality before reality and being able to see in time before time. I always knew that it was more to me than what I was doing and where I was at. While being out in nature it taught me a different form of communication. Repeated numbers, trees, birds, and build boards helped me transcend from beliefs and duality. Walking while feeling inside my imagination so that higher regions of the brain can open as a chakra. Using my emotional energy to move my human body into a different stage.

Two things that are difficult to handle gracefully is failure and success and astray projection allowed me too see the world and control the thoughts of people in the earth world. By being apart of the all knowing, when living day by day I already knew what to expect the day ahead because of my lucid dreaming enabled my travel. So as I'm seeing beyond the ordinary of site and concentration on inner vision brought me bliss. Not only bliss but clarity of the melatonin

formation regulating the reproductive cycle. Clairvoyance an God I feel like your running things in a different dimensions of two. Dollar bill how dare you face life and people still can't see you.

Life can be anything you want it to be if you choose divine knowledge over your regular nine to five job. Besides why waste 62 – 78 mega hurtz of energy under government decisiveness. As they hide our seed of the soul and the magnetic super powers given to us beyond birth. Diagnosis made by man kind with immunizations for the blind. How about sun gazing so that our spiritual side want be left behind. A Pineal Gland enhanced and redesigned for those of us undermined. Thank you God for a higher self your just in time.

Creating a new lifestyle for a new level of consciousness; like a journey from the bottom. Heart to head connection and judging well with discernment. Maybe it's all make believe famous are not; those subliminal messages is just a mock. Entertainment for what you see and hear against the illuminati mysterious spears. Damaging frequent energy high and low with no balance our control. Heavy heart are a light feather which is supremacy measure. Afterlife and a whole lot of treasure.

Shock of the world Nipsey Hussle crossed by a crew. God and the messiah bruised while facing the cruel. That third eye vision made him quick on his feet and good. Risen above like the planets; who's throne is it now. Anunnaki Duel with a name chosen beyond a fire of jewels. Material thing's just has to be left; where a body was stolen God isn't that theft. Dr. Sebi style knowing that his legacy was still addressed.

# Money, Power, Respect

Dear God it seem as though that you have to have money to be respected at a certain level. Criticized from both sides just to provide for children without being admired. Instead of picking cotton our gold was used to make a different currency. A ruled domination replicating different pieces and aspects of America. Golden plates rhythmically placed as extreme value. While the enemy transpire money to make exceptional for man kind to be devour. Too many germs; hand to hand like they're passing out influenza.

You can't benefit from culture if you disrespect our culture. Drugs for soul's and soul's for goals. Who can sell the most stay's free depending on who and what you may know. Genocide melonin people used by government to kill our God like kind. Money too is distributed to low class who was brought into earth to subsidize. Gold is ours paid with a price of riches of blood stamped and approved. No need to join hands with the enemy when in god we trust.

Dead presidents still exist as a bill of rights with the treasury

and federal seal. Lets go back to the old with bricks of gold; no comparison when they're all decomposed. Downtown in any city a federal reserved vault dared to be touched without an exalt. Exposure to power while hiding our foreign knowledge. Included in the bill of rights and we still slave to fight our biggest opposer yet. Yea, lets all fight the right to pick cotton in a different form. Meanwhile it's all transformed with blindness of a platform.

Even the riches of people can become a public enemy of state. With knew gold of knowledge that you can't pay for in college. Tuition and fees charge to learn a ancient history that's free. Non colored people discovering fossils and more parts of Egypt. We will rise despite those who can't handle sunshine. Organs keep them living not races but only God like traces. A chosen gene as if the funeral home dispatched real roses.

No respect of person's just anybody to fulfil life curses. Us as the people crying and hurting like infants before and after shots. Not liquor shots but controlled substances in a liquid form to promote a cause of war. In world were aids and diseases are on tour. All natural products, herbs and essential water, just to make a body of flowers. Starting with the man in the mirror and a made of honor work just has to be done to be empowered. Our father, son & mother nature is love during a wonderful sensation.

# What's Next Knowledge

The difference between a genius and stupidity is that a genius has a limit. God we often hear that it's not what you know it's who you know. But just because you know someone doesn't mean your limited abilities are the same. Understanding of self & from whence thou come will give you the opportunity to know your origins and responsibilities in the world. Each day of our life is giving us a chance to master the monster that is in side of us. All the experts in the world agree only one thing. That they have no idea of the true idea which pursue us daily.

Stone structures found all over the world gives enlightenment of our eternity. Meaning out of body is war for gold. But what is gold? Human gold? Or materialistic gold? Created and master of the divine taking time to unwind golden plates. Projecting alien beings from the place above; in a world of space were there's know such thing as love. Give time and energy into your divinity of chakras. That way today's currency can be traded in as our holy trinity of magic.

Our enemy of mother nature has blind folded us into loosing it, instead of using it. With many weapons going across the globe NASA like. Eighty HD a chemical type just to make our children hype. Through a system that produces a whole lot of white. Medicated and combined for the chemical reaction to they're goal. Leaving 63% to put it up they're nose. 25 mega hurtz stuck on stupid and froze. Reach for the moon and if you miss at least you will end up amongst the stars. Operating on the universe as if it's a game system, his system, your system, they system, our system. Universal God's and Goddesses functioning as self on a planet of water. Unpredictable as to how humans really walk on water. So many different types of water, spiritual water, heavenly water and PH water 9.5 essential style. That makes many of bodies of water covering up 70% of the world. Small things to a giant with a mind locating only on copper. Brain electricity conductivity with a freshly exposed surface, ductile metal, and very high thermal energy.

Subtlety is the art of saying what you think and getting out of the way before it is understood. God it is you who formed us in eternity before the foundations of the world established reincarnation. Each and everyday evil is all around us, making a easy way for negativity to enter our cell membrane. So the art of knowing that no one is perfect makes you become mature in life. Faith is the shield to your destiny; use it to take you places your body can't go. Leaving only one thing in the world more valuable than money and that's knowledge. Knowledge of system's beyond worldly brains moving at a e cycle paste.

# I'am That I'am

Now being chosen by God you can be used to modify that something in particular deserves a specified description. Actually, being chosen stirs up fear on the inside. Knowing that God has called you too do things of nature that no one but you can do. Which is why the enemy focuses more on the way they look on the outside; than the way God created us on the inside. If you plant a peach seed everything that the peach needs to make it great is already in the seed. Meanwhile in that seed is more seed's to reproduce more peaches. That economically benefits everyone involved if you have the know how to reproduce. A system that is controlling the way you speak the way you understand and how you think.

When you were a child you spoke as a child, you understood as a child and you thought as a child. But when you became a growing being things of a child got put away. Childlike behavior functioning on the inside as immature behavior. Blaming of self for things that's out of our control. Allowing a system to put you away because you

can not put it away. Mixing of priorities and not focused enough to know which is right from wrong. Never climb a mountain with excess bagged on your back, and always be willing to release the unknown.

A eating of self; while chicken's turn into birds and bird's turn into eagles. Being Gun down flying in the sky a moment in time where bullets is just a spy. Different dimensions of self-flowing like a river till you reach your destiny. There you'll meet jealousy and hatred with evil deeds of dark sprits. Magic of envy maybe using candles and prayers blooming like flowers. Bed bug biting for just a little enlightenment. Sad how love just a little tool to lock the brain in a way of thinking so that molecules can operate.

How can you love God whom you never seen and hate your neighbor whom you seen? The enemy will attack your mind that affects your physical well being. Next step is the body and flesh is just flesh with know spirit of operation until a knowing of self has manifested. Once you began to know yourself powers began to unlock as if keys has been dispatched. Chakras techniques that the universe can use as a gift to go within side of you. Not asking for pleads and deals with different blood types of human itself. Being played as if you're blood type isn't ordained in laboratory works. So that you can be reincarnated through self not of blood but of spirit.

What's more to learn about self when time is just a essential package delivered with obstacle's. To prevent a true learning lets distract each other within each other. Using words as a knife to damage the soul with negative energy as mind control. Happens to the best of us when we all playing in different roles. Glued to the earth like a race to space. Killers and killings of many from far away like God this is how they say they're grace. No, thanks to those of another race I must look above and head for another home base.

# *Go On*

God I must pick my feet up and go on in time. It's like a enemy of
your divine as I continue to face everything that's next for me to
subside. In hurt and pain like a wounded warrior with battles that I
might have strength for but still doesn't defeat. Go on & die just to
see how it feel; like animals at night hunting in the field. You, me
and the rest of them, got seven senses why not go on what's the big
deal? Survivor of the fittest with different agendas. Invisible armor
that blind eyes can't even see and light from the moon has got owl
eyes in misbelief. Another sense coming in at full speed this enemy
has to be listening to me.

New level's to beat mountains with very high peaks and I still
must remain petite. Over the limit standing like boom" one bomb
now I'm in between earth, the moon & the universe. What a site
to see as many will talk in mischief towards those that's over seas.
Vacation or journey or maybe it's make believe to go on with life in a
new dimension. Third degree burns & scars I still can't feel how pain

feel when you orbit throughout the stars. Friends and family I still can see after I close my eyes and go to sleep. Back awake walking in the sunshine with a grand awakening and many cross minds.

After life and rebirth with children of the universe alienated until human form. Right back to life bills and people who could of came in misconstrued. A purpose to be scene as many kings and queens wait one after another to be the greatest one to make it. In a generation of like minds but know cooperation. A bigger enemy fighting us all and is dedicated to medicated blood of choice. Feet stamped at birthed you've been noticed and cursed. Not by your mind enemy this battle is inclusive and the only way to figure it out is too teleport.

Go on and transcend out of sight out of mind you'll be able to come back alive. Like you never fell down and had to go through trails and tribulations just to reset. But now your strong enough to charge ahead with powers of life untold and said. Come on now everybody is not scared of the new world order that's has now interfered with our manifestation. A new raising of plants and crops; watched over by mirrored rain and infant red beam lights. Sun energy gained to beat the virus itself why stay in and quarantine. Who do you really trust?

In god we trust a planet itself; not by money neither nor dust. You said dodged a bullet twice but each and every day is a gamble at life. Bath in the tub lets wash these demons off in return for a skin faded like snakes when sheading off. New face and look which is magic itself. How come it's so much hate and only one rep? God himself visualizing our lives to come & masturbating earth with a new dawn. Dreams do come true like a miracle child unnoticed till born at a pound. Shot at life speeding recovery for all mansions and life's discoveries.

# About the Author

Danyell Todd began her unknown journey the day that she was born. Born on February 10, 1992 to Janice Courtney and Donyell Todd Sr; who was captured into the struggle in the Darst- Webbe Peabody Projects. Having a disturbing childhood, both of her parents still survived with four children and an on/off relationship amongst the two. Physically losing her dad June 2008 changed her life forever because she started wondering who God really was. No one had ever mentioned God to her until she was able to understand higher power of herself.

Living a daily life and facing common obstacles made her realize that it was more to life than hardships and struggle. She then started writing letters to God expressing her inner thoughts and compassions. Not knowing that she was writing out her life's purpose and who she should become. In a planet of worlds orchestrated by God while being divided amongst a few. Powerless until power is giving by birthing knowledge in a brain circumcision to a bird's eye view.

Printed in the United States
By Bookmasters